soups

soups

This edition first published in the U.K. in 1999 by Hamlyn for WHSmith, Greenbridge Road, Swindon SN3 3LD

Octopus Publishing Group Limited
2–4 Heron Quays
London E14 4JP

ISBN 0600 59973 6

Printed in Hong Kong

Notes

1 Standard level spoon measurements are used in all recipes.

1 tablespoon = one 15 ml spoon
1 teaspoon = one 5 ml spoon

2 Both imperial and metric measurements have been given in all recipes. Use one set of measurements only and not a mixture of both.

3 Measurements for canned food have been given as a standard metric equivalent.

4 Eggs should be medium unless otherwise stated. The Department of Health advises that eggs should not be consumed raw. This book may contain dishes made with lightly cooked eggs. It is prudent for more vulnerable people, such as pregnant and nursing mothers, invalids, the elderly, babies and young children, to avoid uncooked or lightly cooked dishes made with eggs. Once prepared, these dishes should be used immediately.

5 Milk should be full fat unless otherwise stated.

6 Poultry should be cooked thoroughly. To test if poultry is cooked, pierce the flesh through the thickest part with a skewer or fork – the juices should run clear, never pink or red.

7 Fresh herbs should be used unless otherwise stated. If unavailable, use dried herbs as an alternative but halve the quantities stated.

8 Pepper should be freshly ground black pepper unless otherwise stated; season according to taste.

9 Ovens should be preheated to the specified temperature – if using a fan-assisted oven, follow the manufacturer's instructions for adjusting the time and the temperature.

10 Do not refreeze a dish that has been frozen previously.

11 This book includes dishes made with nuts and nut derivatives. It is advisable for customers with known allergic reactions to nuts and nut derivatives and those who may be potentially vulnerable to these allergies, such as pregnant and nursing mothers, invalids, the elderly, babies and children, to avoid dishes made with nuts and nut oils. It is also prudent to check the labels of pre-prepared ingredients for the possible inclusion of nut derivatives.

12 Vegetarians should look for the 'V' symbol on a cheese to ensure it is made with vegetarian rennet. There are vegetarian forms of Parmesan, feta, Cheddar, Cheshire, red Leicester, dolcelatte and many goats' cheeses, among others.

These delicious and filling soups from all corners of the world can be served as a meal in themselves. Serve them with a variety of breads such as French bread, Italian ciabatta, garlic bread or crusty rolls to make a nutritious and satisfying lunch or supper.

This selection of mouthwatering soups has something for every occasion. Try the homely Smoked Haddock Chowder as a family starter or the sophisticated Mussel Soup with Saffron, Basil and Spinach as a first course to delight your dinner party guests.

Whether the soup requires everyday vegetables such as carrots or cauliflower, or more exotic ingredients, like Jerusalem artichokes or sweet potatoes, these recipes produce tantalising results. Most of these soups are ideal for vegetarians – just make sure that vegetable stock is used, with a vegetarian cheese, when needed.

There is nothing more refreshing on a hot summer's day than a chilled soup. This chapter contains both fresh savoury soups and invigorating fruit soups, all of which are perfect partners for relaxed summer *al fresco* dining.

contents

introduction

Soup is an amazingly versatile dish. While nothing is more welcome than a hearty vegetable broth on a cold winter's evening, a delicately flavoured chilled soup makes a deliciously refreshing summer lunch. Creamy soups have a sophisticated richness of flavour that makes them perfect for a dinner party.

Making soup is surprisingly easy. It is always worth buying the best quality ingredients and using a good stock. Fresh herbs are always preferable to dried. Use a large, heavy-based saucepan so that the ingredients do not stick to the base and there is plenty of room to stir the soup. Serve hot soup in a warmed tureen or warmed bowls. Chill the bowls for serving iced soups.

Stock

Although stock or bouillon cubes may be satisfactory and convenient for some types of dishes, a good-quality stock is essential for really successful soup. The flavour is incomparable and you are in control of the seasoning – most stock cubes tend to be quite salty. The ingredients for stock are inexpensive and it is very easy to make. Packs of chicken trimmings and bones for stock are available from most supermarkets and can be bought from the butcher. Fish trimmings are also available and, if you are buying fresh fish from a fishmonger, always ask for the head and trimmings from fish to be filleted and use them for making stock.

Four stock recipes follow and these form the basis of almost all the recipes in this book. Beef stock is a rich brown colour and is ideal for meaty soups and those made with strongly flavoured vegetables. It requires long, slow cooking, but is worth it. Chicken stock, which can be made from raw trimmings or the carcass of a cooked chicken, is a good all-purpose stock. Fish stock is quite delicately flavoured and very quickly made. It is ideal for fish and seafood soups, although chicken stock may be substituted. Vegetable stock is quite light and is perfect for aromatic vegetable soups. You can use virtually any vegetables you like, but avoid floury root vegetables, such as potatoes, as they will make the stock cloudy. Add tomatoes for extra richness and a sliver of orange or lemon rind for an extra lift.

Never try to hurry stock. It needs to simmer very gently or it will evaporate too quickly and go cloudy. Do not add salt to the stock because as it reduces, the flavours concentrate and it might become too salty. Season with salt when making the soup. Always remove the scum that rises to the surface using a skimmer or slotted spoon. Once it is cooked, strain the stock – ideally, through a muslin-lined sieve – and allow to cool completely before storing in the refrigerator. A layer of fat will usually form on the surface of cold beef and chicken stock. Remove and discard this before using. All stocks freeze well. You can store them in plastic tubs or freeze them in ice cube trays and then pack in freezer bags for ease of storage.

beef stock

1 Put the bones in a roasting tin and cook in a preheated oven, 230°C (450°F), Gas Mark 8, for about 1 hour, or until just browned and the fat and juices have run out. Using a slotted spoon, transfer the bones to a large saucepan.

2 Place the roasting tin over a low heat. Add the onions, carrots and celery and fry, stirring frequently, for 10 minutes, until browned. Add the vegetables to the pan, together with the bay leaves, parsley, thyme and peppercorns. Pour in the water.

3 Bring to the boil and skim off any scum that rises to the surface. Lower the heat and simmer, skimming the surface occasionally, for 8 hours. Strain and cool, then chill in the refrigerator. Remove any fat from the surface before using.

2.5 kg (5 lb) beef bones or beef and veal bones

2 onions, roughly chopped

2 carrots, roughly chopped

2 celery sticks, roughly chopped

2 bay leaves

3–4 parsley sprigs

2 thyme sprigs

10 black peppercorns

4.8 litres (8 pints) cold water

Makes about 2.7 litres (4½ pints)

Preparation time: 5–10 minutes

Cooking time: about 9 hours

chicken stock

1 Chop the chicken carcass into 3–4 pieces and place in a large saucepan, together with the giblets and trimmings. Add the carrots, onion, celery, herbs and water and bring to the boil, skimming off any scum that rises to the surface.

2 Lower the heat and simmer, skimming the surface occasionally, for 2–2½ hours. Strain through a muslin-lined sieve, set aside to cool completely, then store in the refrigerator.

cooked chicken carcass, plus raw giblets and trimmings

2 large carrots, roughly chopped

1 onion, roughly chopped

1 celery stick, roughly chopped

1 thyme sprig

1 bay leaf

4–6 parsley sprigs, lightly crushed

1.8 litres (3 pints) cold water

Makes 1 litre (1¾ pints)

Preparation time: 5–10 minutes

Cooking time: about 2½ hours

fish stock

1 Put all the ingredients in a large saucepan and bring to just below boiling point over a low heat. Simmer for 20 minutes, skimming off any scum that rises to the surface.

2 Strain the stock through a muslin-lined sieve. Set aside to cool completely, then store in the refrigerator.

1.5 kg (3 lb) fish heads and trimmings

1 onion, sliced

1 carrot, sliced

1 small leek, white part only

1 celery stick

1 bay leaf

1 thyme sprig

6 parsley sprigs

10 black peppercorns

475 ml (16 fl oz) dry white wine

1.8 litres (3 pints) cold water

Makes 1.8 litres (3 pints)

Preparation time: 10 minutes

Cooking time: 20 minutes

■ All white fish are suitable for making stock, but avoid using oily fish, such as mackerel or herrings. You can also use the heads and shells of seafood, such as prawns.

vegetable stock

1 Put all the ingredients in a large saucepan and bring to the boil over a moderate heat. Lower the heat and simmer for 30 minutes, skimming off any scum that rises to the surface.

2 Strain the stock through a muslin-lined sieve. Set aside to cool completely, then store in the refrigerator.

500 g (1 lb) mixed vegetables, such as equal quantities of carrots, leeks, celery, onion and mushrooms, chopped

1 garlic clove

6 black peppercorns

1 bouquet garni (2 parsley sprigs, 2 thyme sprigs and 1 bay leaf)

1.2 litres (2 pints) cold water

Makes 1 litre (1¾ pints)

Preparation time: 5–10 minutes

Cooking time: 45 minutes

'Only the pure of heart can make a good soup.'

Ludwig van Beethoven

Garnishes

There are many simple ways to make your soups look as wonderful as they taste. Add a swirl of soured cream, crème fraîche or natural yogurt just before serving. Drawing a cocktail stick gently through the swirl creates a delicate feathered effect. Sprinkle the soup with snipped chives or tiny herb sprigs, such as dill or flat leaf parsley. Croûtons and crispy fried diced bacon add a delicious contrast in texture to creamy soups.

To make croûtons, remove the crusts from 50 g (2 oz) day-old white bread and cut the bread into small squares. Fry over a moderate heat in 2 tablespoons vegetable oil or 50 g (2 oz) butter, stirring and tossing constantly. Vary the flavour by adding garlic, anchovies, bacon or cheese.

Tomatoes

When using tomatoes to make soup it is best to skin them first. To do this, cut a small cross in the base of each tomato, place in a bowl and cover with boiling water. Within 10–15 seconds, the skins will begin to roll back. Remove the tomatoes and refresh them in iced water, then peel off the skins.

rocket & white bean twin soup
with basil & walnut pesto •
mulligatawny soup •
armenian onion & lentil soup •
quick chestnut & bacon soup •
coconut & plantain soup •
bean soup •
pumpkin, garlic & peanut butter soup •
spanish chickpea soup •
risi e bisi with frazzled prosciutto •
pronto provençal soup •
white cabbage soup with meatballs •
goulash soup •
potato & bacon soup •
bean thread noodle soup •
cream of chicken soup •
speedy watercress soup with poached quails' eggs •

hearty
soups

rocket & white bean twin soup with basil & walnut pesto

1 To make the white bean soup, drain and rinse the haricot or cannellini beans and place in a saucepan with the water. Bring to the boil, reduce the heat and simmer for 45–60 minutes, or until tender. Transfer the beans, together with the cooking liquid, to a blender or food processor, in batches if necessary, and process to a purée. Strain through a sieve, pressing with the back of a ladle to extract as much soup as possible. Return the soup to the pan and season to taste with salt and pepper.

2 To make the pesto, place the basil, parsley, walnuts and garlic in a blender or food processor and process until finely chopped. With the motor running, gradually add the oil in a thin stream until fully incorporated. Scrape the pesto into a bowl, stir in the Parmesan and season to taste with salt and pepper.

3 To make the rocket soup, melt the butter in a large saucepan. Add the onion and cook over a low heat, stirring occasionally, for 5–6 minutes, until softened, but not coloured. Add the potatoes, stir, cover and cook for 5 minutes. Add the rocket, cover and cook for 3–4 minutes, stirring occasionally, until just wilted. Add the stock and milk, season to taste with salt and pepper and simmer for 10 minutes, until the potatoes are tender. Process the soup in a blender or food processor, in batches if necessary. Strain through a sieve into a clean saucepan.

4 Reheat the soups separately. Add the double cream to the rocket soup, heat gently without boiling and adjust the seasoning to taste. Adjust the consistency of the white bean soup, by adding more water or stock if needed, so that it is the same consistency as the rocket soup. Using 2 ladles, simultaneously pour the soups into warmed individual soup bowls. Serve drizzled with the basil and walnut pesto.

White Bean Soup:

250 g (8 oz) dried haricot or cannellini beans, soaked overnight

900 ml (1½ pints) cold water

salt and pepper

Basil & Walnut Pesto:

25 g (1 oz) basil leaves

15 g (½ oz) flat leaf parsley

25 g (1 oz) walnuts

2 garlic cloves, chopped

125 ml (4 fl oz) extra virgin olive oil

25 g (1 oz) Parmesan cheese, finely grated

Rocket Soup:

25 g (1 oz) butter

1 onion, chopped

2 potatoes, about 250 g (8 oz), cut into 1.5 cm (¾ inch) dice

200 g (7 oz) rocket, roughly chopped

300 ml (½ pint) Chicken or Vegetable Stock (see pages 7 and 8)

300 ml (½ pint) milk

100 ml (3½ fl oz) double cream

Serves 4
Preparation time: 45 minutes, plus overnight soaking
Cooking time: 45–60 minutes

mulligatawny soup

1 Heat the oil in a heavy-based saucepan. Add the onions and fry, stirring occasionally, until browned. Stir in the curry powder and cook, stirring occasionally, for 2 minutes. Add the garlic, lentils, red pepper, chillies, stock, raisins and tomatoes and season with salt and pepper to taste. Bring to the boil, lower the heat, cover and simmer for 1½ hours.

2 Remove the pan from the heat and set aside to cool slightly. Sieve the soup or process in a blender or food processor until smooth. Return to the pan and heat through.

3 Ladle the soup into warmed soup bowls, garnish with saffron rice, if liked, and serve immediately.

2 tablespoons vegetable oil

2 large onions, chopped

1 tablespoon curry powder

2 garlic cloves, crushed

250 g (8 oz) green lentils, washed and drained

1 red pepper, cored, deseeded and chopped

3 dried chillies, chopped

1.2 litres (2 pints) Chicken Stock (see page 7)

25 g (1 oz) seedless raisins

250 g (8 oz) tomatoes, skinned (see page 9), deseeded and chopped

1 tablespoon tomato purée

salt and pepper

saffron rice (see below), to garnish (optional)

Serves 8
Preparation time: 10 minutes
Cooking time: 1¾ hours

■ To make saffron rice, cook 2-3 tablespoons of long-grain rice in boiling salted water, with a few strands of saffron, for 15 minutes, until tender.

1 Put the barley into a saucepan with the water. Bring the mixture to the boil. Lower the heat, partially cover and simmer, stirring occasionally, for 25–30 minutes, or until all the water is absorbed.

2 Add the stock, onions, lentils, tarragon, paprika, cayenne, sugar and wine. Bring the mixture to the boil, lower the heat, partially cover and simmer for about 1¼ hours. Add more water if the soup is too thick. Season to taste with salt and pepper.

3 For the garnish, melt the butter or margarine in a small frying pan over a moderate heat. Add the onion and cook, stirring occasionally, for 5 minutes, or until soft and golden.

4 Carefully ladle the soup into warmed bowls, garnish with the fried onion and serve immediately.

25 g (1 oz) pearl barley

150 ml (¼ pint) water

1.8 litres (3 pints) Beef Stock (see page 7)

500 g (1 lb) onions, thinly sliced

150 g (5 oz) green lentils, washed and drained

1 teaspoon dried tarragon

2 teaspoons paprika

pinch of cayenne pepper

¼ teaspoon sugar

3 tablespoons dry white wine

salt and pepper

To Garnish:

25 g (1 oz) butter or margarine

3 tablespoons finely chopped mild onion

Serves 8
Preparation time: 15 minutes
Cooking time: about 1¾ hours

armenian onion & lentil soup

quick chestnut & bacon soup

1 Melt the butter in a large, heavy-based saucepan over a moderate heat. Add the bacon and cook, stirring occasionally, for 2–3 minutes, until lightly browned. Reduce the heat and add the shallots or onion, fennel and celery and cook for 6–8 minutes, until softened.

2 Add the chestnuts to the pan, together with the stock and milk and season to taste with salt and pepper. Bring to the boil, reduce the heat and simmer for 15–20 minutes, until the chestnuts are tender.

3 Meanwhile, prepare the croûtes. Rub the ciabatta slices with the garlic halves. Pour the olive oil into a small plate, dip the bread in the oil and place under a preheated hot grill until toasted to light golden.

4 Process the soup in a blender or food processor, in batches if necessary. Strain through a sieve, return to the pan and bring back to the boil. Ladle into warm serving bowls, add a swirl of cream to each and serve with the garlic croûtes.

50 g (2 oz) butter

75 g (3 oz) bacon, rinded and chopped

3 shallots or 1 large onion, chopped

½ small fennel bulb, chopped

1 celery stick, chopped

250 g (8 oz) vacuum-packed cooked chestnuts

600 ml (1 pint) Chicken or Vegetable Stock (see pages 7 and 8)

600 ml (1 pint) milk

salt and pepper

double cream, to serve

Croûtes:

8 slices ciabatta

2 garlic cloves, cut in half

75 ml (3 fl oz) extra virgin olive oil

Serves 4
Preparation time: 15 minutes
Cooking time: 25–35 minutes

■ Ciabatta is a rustic Italian bread made with olive oil and often flavoured with herbs, olives or sun-dried tomatoes. The texture is light and the crust is crisp.

coconut & plantain soup

1 Heat the oil in a large saucepan. Add the onion, garlic, chilli, ginger and lime rind and cook, stirring occasionally, for 8–10 minutes, until softened. Add the tomatoes and cook for a further 5 minutes.

2 To peel the plantains, cut off one end and, using a small sharp knife, slit the skin down its length, then peel it off sideways. Chop the flesh and add to the pan, together with the allspice, thyme, stock and coconut milk. Season to taste with salt and pepper, bring to the boil, reduce the heat and simmer for 30 minutes until the plantains are tender.

3 Meanwhile, place the Brazil nuts on a baking sheet and place in a preheated oven, 160°C (325°F), Gas Mark 3, for 10–15 minutes, until light golden. Remove from the oven, set aside to cool, then chop finely.

4 Remove the soup from the heat and discard the thyme sprig. Process the soup in a blender or food processor, in batches if necessary. Strain through a sieve and return to the pan to reheat. Add the lime juice and adjust the seasoning to taste. Serve in warmed bowls sprinkled with the chopped Brazil nuts.

2 tablespoons vegetable oil

1 onion, finely chopped

1–2 garlic cloves, crushed

1 fresh red chilli, deseeded and finely chopped

2.5 cm (1 inch) piece of fresh root ginger, grated

finely grated rind and juice of 1 lime

2 tomatoes, about 300 g (10 oz), skinned (see page 9) and chopped

2 large semi–ripe plantains or green bananas

6 allspice berries, crushed

1 thyme sprig

1.2 litres (2 pints) Chicken Stock (see page 7)

400 ml (14 fl oz) can unsweetened coconut milk

salt and pepper

75 g (3 oz) shelled Brazil nuts, to serve

Serves 6

Preparation time: 20 minutes

Cooking time: 45 minutes

1 Drain the haricot and kidney beans, rinse in cold water and drain again. Put them into a large saucepan, cover with cold water and bring to the boil. Boil vigorously for 10 minutes, then lower the heat, cover and simmer for 1¼ hours, or until the beans are tender. Drain and set aside.

2 Melt the butter in a large, heavy-based saucepan. Add the onions and fry over a medium heat for 5–6 minutes, until golden. Add the garlic, celery, carrots, peas, tomatoes, together with their can juice, wine, stock and bouquet garni and season with salt and pepper to taste. Bring to the boil, lower the heat, cover and simmer for 20 minutes.

3 Stir in the courgettes, Worcestershire sauce and tomato purée. Continue cooking for 5 minutes, then add the cooked beans and heat through.

4 Meanwhile, make the pistou. Pound the garlic, basil, oil and nuts to a smooth paste using a mortar and a pestle. Mix the pistou into the soup just before serving.

125 g (4 oz) haricot beans, soaked overnight in cold water to cover

50 g (2 oz) red kidney beans, soaked overnight in cold water to cover

25 g (1 oz) butter

2 large onions, chopped

2 garlic cloves, crushed

2 celery sticks, chopped

2 large carrots, chopped

50 g (2 oz) fresh peas or frozen peas, defrosted

425 g (14 oz) can tomatoes

125 ml (4 fl oz) dry red wine

300 ml (½ pint) Chicken Stock (see page 7)

1 bouquet garni

125 g (4 oz) courgettes, sliced

1 tablespoon Worcestershire sauce

1 tablespoon tomato purée

salt and pepper

Pistou:

4 garlic cloves

1 bunch basil

4 tablespoons olive oil

25 g (1 oz) pine nuts

Serves 6–8

Preparation time: 20 minutes, plus soaking

Cooking time: 2½ hours

bean soup

pumpkin, garlic & peanut butter soup

1 To make the breadsticks, sift the flour and salt into the bowl of a food processor, add the yeast, oil and chilli. With the machine running, gradually add enough water to form a soft dough. Turn the dough on to a lightly floured surface and knead for 5 minutes, until smooth and elastic. Divide the dough into 16 pieces and roll each into a stick about 28 cm (11 inches) long and 1 cm (½ inch) thick. Place on a lightly oiled baking sheet and leave to rise for 15–20 minutes. Bake in a preheated oven, 150°C (300°F), Gas Mark 2, for 1 hour, until lightly browned and crisp.

2 Increase the oven temperature to 180°C (350°F), Gas Mark 4. Place the garlic cloves in a baking tin and toss with 1 tablespoon of the oil. Cook for 15–20 minutes, until softened. Leave to cool then pop the soft flesh out of the skins and reserve.

3 Heat the remaining oil in a large, heavy-based saucepan. Add the onion, celery and leek and cook over a low heat, stirring frequently, for 8–10 minutes, until softened. Add all the remaining ingredients, including the baked garlic cloves, bring to the boil and simmer for 20–30 minutes, until the vegetables are soft. Remove and discard the bay leaf and thyme.

4 Process the soup in a blender or food processor. Strain through a sieve, return to the pan and bring back to the boil. Top each bowl of soup with a spoonful of soured cream or crème fraîche, and serve accompanied by the chilli breadsticks.

6–8 garlic cloves, unpeeled

3 tablespoons olive oil

1 large onion, chopped

2 celery sticks, chopped

1 leek, chopped

6 allspice berries, crushed

1 thyme sprig

1 bay leaf

2 tomatoes, skinned (see page 9) and chopped

50 g (2 oz) peanut butter

750 g (1½ lb) peeled pumpkin, cubed

1.5 litres (2½ pints) Chicken Stock (see page 7)

salt and pepper

200 ml (7 fl oz) soured cream or crème fraîche, to serve

Chilli Breadsticks:

250 g (8 oz) plain flour

½ teaspoon salt

4½ teaspoons easy-blend dried yeast

1 tablespoon olive oil

1 fresh red or green chilli, deseeded and very finely chopped

about 175 ml (6 fl oz) warm water

Serves 4–6
Preparation time: 45 minutes
Cooking time: 1 hour 40 minutes

spanish chickpea soup

1   Drain the chickpeas, rinse under cold water and drain again. Put the bacon joint in a deep saucepan and cover with cold water. Bring the water to the boil, then drain the bacon, discarding the water.

2   Return the bacon joint to the clean saucepan. Add the chickpeas, onion, garlic, bay leaf, thyme, marjoram, parsley and the water. Bring the mixture to the boil, then lower the heat, partially cover and simmer for 1½ hours. Remove and discard the onion, bay leaf and herb sprigs. Lift out the bacon, cut it into small pieces and set aside.

3   Add the stock, potatoes and cabbage to the pan and simmer for a further 30 minutes. Add the reserved bacon pieces to the soup and cook for a further 10 minutes. Season with salt and pepper to taste. Serve in warmed soup bowls.

150 g (5 oz) dried chickpeas, covered with boiling water and soaked overnight

1 small boneless smoked bacon hock joint, about 500–750 g (1–1½ lb)

1 onion, studded with 4 cloves

2 garlic cloves, crushed

1 bay leaf

1 thyme sprig

1 marjoram sprig

1 parsley sprig

1.8 litres (3 pints) water

1.8 litres (3 pints) Chicken Stock (see page 7)

300–375 g (10–12 oz) potatoes, cut into 1 cm (½ inch) cubes

300 g (10 oz) Savoy cabbage, shredded

salt and pepper

Serves 8–10

Preparation time: 15 minutes, plus soaking

Cooking time: 2½–2¾ hours

1 Pod the peas. Heat the oil in a large, heavy-based saucepan over a medium heat. Add the onion and cook, stirring, for 5–10 minutes, until softened but not coloured.

2 Add the stock, bring to the boil, reduce the heat and add the peas. Simmer gently for 5 minutes then stir in the rice. Season with salt, pepper and a pinch of sugar. Cover and simmer gently, stirring occasionally, for 15–20 minutes, until the rice is tender.

3 For the garnish, cut each slice of prosciutto in half lengthways. Heat the oil in a large frying pan, add the prosciutto strips and fry over a high heat for 10–15 seconds, until crisp. Drain on kitchen paper.

4 Stir the parsley and Parmesan into the hot soup. Serve the soup in individual bowls, each topped with 2 pieces of the frazzled prosciutto. Serve a small bowl of extra grated Parmesan separately.

750 g (1½ lb) fresh young peas in the pod

3 tablespoons olive oil

1 onion, chopped

1.2 litres (2 pints) Chicken Stock (see page 7)

200 g (7 oz) risotto rice

large pinch of sugar

2 tablespoons chopped flat leaf parsley

50 g (2 oz) Parmesan cheese, finely grated, plus extra to serve

salt and pepper

To Garnish:

4 slices of prosciutto

1 tablespoon olive oil

Serves 4	
Preparation time: 10 minutes	
Cooking time: 25–40 minutes	

risi e bisi with frazzled prosciutto

pronto
provençal
soup

1 First prepare the garnish. Cut the tomatoes in half lengthways and, holding them over a bowl, scoop out the seeds with a spoon; reserve the seeds. Place the tomato halves on a lightly oiled baking sheet. Mix together the garlic, oil and salt and drizzle over the tomatoes. Place in a preheated oven, 150°C (300°F), Gas Mark 2, for 30 minutes.

2 Meanwhile, heat the oil in a large saucepan over a low heat. Add the onion and garlic and cook, stirring occasionally, for 5–10 minutes, until softened, but not coloured. Add the peppers, aubergine and courgettes and cook for a further 10 minutes. Add the tomatoes with the reserved seeds and juice from the plum tomatoes, the vinegar, stock, thyme and coriander seeds. Bring to the boil, reduce the heat and simmer for 15–20 minutes. Add the olives after 10–15 minutes. Season to taste with salt and pepper.

3 To finish the garnish, mix the cheese with the chopped parsley and a pinch of cayenne pepper. Remove the tomatoes from the oven and place a spoonful of the cheese mixture in each. Return to the oven for 5–10 minutes, until the cheese is melted and bubbling.

4 Reheat the soup, if necessary, and stir in the parsley and basil. Pour into individual bowls and top each with 2 baked tomato halves.

4 tablespoons extra virgin olive oil

1 large onion, chopped

1 garlic clove, crushed

1 small red pepper, cored, deseeded and cut into 1 cm (½ inch) cubes

1 small yellow pepper, cored, deseeded and cut into 1 cm (½ inch) cubes

1 aubergine, about 300 g (10 oz), cut into 1 cm (½ inch) cubes

2 courgettes, about 250 g (8 oz), cut into 1 cm (½ inch) cubes

4 tomatoes, about 300 g (10 oz), skinned (see page 9) and chopped

1 tablespoon wine vinegar

450 ml (¾ pint) Chicken or Vegetable Stock (see pages 7 and 8)

1 thyme sprig

½ teaspoon coriander seeds, crushed

50 g (2 oz) pitted black olives, chopped

2 tablespoons chopped parsley

1 tablespoon chopped basil

salt and pepper

To Garnish:

4 large plum tomatoes

1 small garlic clove, crushed

1 tablespoon olive oil, plus extra for greasing

¼ teaspoon salt

50 g (2 oz) Gruyère or fontina cheese, finely grated

1 tablespoon chopped parsley

cayenne pepper

Serves 4
Preparation time: 25 minutes
Cooking time: 30–40 minutes

white cabbage soup with meatballs

1 Melt the butter or margarine in a large, heavy-based saucepan. Add the cabbage and sugar and cook, stirring constantly, until the cabbage is golden. Add the stock, allspice and peppercorns. Lower the heat, cover and simmer for 30–35 minutes, or until the cabbage is tender. Season with salt to taste.

2 To make the meatballs, place the breadcrumbs in a bowl, add the water and set aside to soak for 3 minutes. Then add the veal, pork, egg yolks, salt, pepper, Worcestershire sauce and Dijon mustard. Stir the mixture vigorously with a fork until it is very smooth. Shape the mixture into balls the size of walnuts between the palms of your hands.

3 Bring the soup to the boil and add the meatballs one at a time. Lower the heat and simmer gently, uncovered, for 10 minutes. Transfer the soup to a warmed tureen and serve immediately.

50 g (2 oz) butter or margarine

1 white cabbage, about 875 g (1¾ lb), coarsely shredded

2 teaspoons sugar

1.5 litres (2½ pints) Beef Stock (see page 7)

3 allspice berries

6 white peppercorns

salt

Meatballs:

2 tablespoons dried white breadcrumbs

150 ml (¼ pint) water

250 g (8 oz) lean minced veal

250 g (8 oz) lean minced pork

2 egg yolks

1 teaspoon salt

¼ teaspoon freshly ground white pepper

1 teaspoon Worcestershire sauce

1 teaspoon Dijon mustard

Serves 4–6
Preparation time: 25 minutes
Cooking time: 45–50 minutes

3 tablespoons vegetable oil

750 g (1½ lb) boneless lean braising steak, cut into 2.5 cm (1 inch) cubes

2 onions, chopped

2 garlic cloves, crushed

2 celery sticks, chopped

3 tablespoons paprika

1 tablespoon caraway seeds

1.2 litres (2 pints) Beef Stock (see page 7)

600 ml (1 pint) water

¼ teaspoon dried thyme

2 bay leaves

¼ teaspoon Tabasco sauce

3 tablespoons tomato purée

350 g (8 oz) potatoes, cut into 1 cm (½ inch) dice

3 carrots, cut into 1 cm (½ inch) dice

6–8 teaspoons soured cream, to garnish (optional)

Serves 6–8

Preparation time: 10–15 minutes

Cooking time: 1¼ hours

---

1 Heat the oil in a heavy-based saucepan. Add the beef, in batches, and brown over a moderate heat. As each batch browns, transfer it to kitchen paper to drain. Then cook the onions, garlic and celery in the oil until transparent.

2 Remove the saucepan from the heat and stir in the paprika, caraway seeds, stock and water. Add the thyme, bay leaves, Tabasco sauce and tomato purée, stir well then add the cooked beef. Bring the mixture to the boil, then lower the heat, partially cover and simmer for 30 minutes.

3 Add the diced potatoes and carrots and simmer for a further 30 minutes, or until the potatoes are tender. Remove and discard the bay leaves. Serve the soup immediately in warmed bowls, garnishing each portion with a teaspoon of soured cream, if liked.

goulash soup

potato & bacon soup

1 Cut the rinds off the bacon and set them aside. Coarsely chop the bacon rashers. Heat the oil in a heavy-based saucepan, add the bacon rinds and cook over a moderate heat until crisp. Remove them with a slotted spoon and discard.

2 Add the chopped bacon, onion and garlic to the pan and cook over a moderate heat, stirring frequently, for 8–10 minutes, or until the onion is light brown and the bacon is fairly crisp. Add the stock, water, potatoes, leeks, cabbage, marjoram, nutmeg and Worcestershire sauce and season with pepper to taste. Bring the mixture to the boil. Lower the heat, cover and simmer, stirring occasionally, for 25 minutes.

3 Process 600 ml (1 pint) of the soup mixture in a blender or food processor for about 2 seconds, then return to the pan. Stir well and cook the soup for a further 10 minutes over a low heat. Season with salt to taste. Just before serving, stir in the parsley, if using. Serve in individual warmed soup bowls.

175 g (6 oz) rashers of smoked bacon

1 tablespoon olive oil

1 onion, finely chopped

2 garlic cloves, finely chopped

600 ml (1 pint) Chicken Stock (see page 7)

1.2 litres (2 pints) water

750 g (1½ lb) potatoes, diced

3 leeks, sliced

300 g (10 oz) cabbage, shredded

1 teaspoon chopped marjoram

¼ teaspoon ground nutmeg

1 teaspoon Worcestershire sauce

3–4 tablespoons finely chopped parsley (optional)

salt and pepper

Serves 8

Preparation time: 20 minutes

Cooking time: 1 hour

bean thread noodle· soup

1 To make the garlic mixture, pound the garlic, coriander and pepper using a mortar and pestle. Heat the oil in a wok or deep frying pan, add the garlic mixture and stir-fry for 1 minute.

2 Add the minced pork and stir-fry for 3 minutes, then pour in the stock and bring to the boil. Stir in the noodles, spring onions, onion, fish sauce and salt. Bring the soup back to the boil and cook for 3 minutes. Lower the heat, add the prawns and celery and simmer for a further 2 minutes.

3 Transfer to a warmed serving bowl, season with pepper and serve immediately.

2 tablespoons vegetable oil

250 g (8 oz) minced pork

1 litre (1¾ pints) Chicken Stock (see page 7)

125 g (4 oz) bean thread noodles

4 spring onions, cut into 2.5 cm (1 inch) lengths

½ onion, finely chopped

2 tablespoons fish sauce

2 tablespoons salt

250 g (8 oz) uncooked prawns, peeled and deveined

2 celery sticks with leaves, chopped

pepper

Garlic Mixture:

1 garlic clove, crushed

1 teaspoon chopped coriander stem

¼ teaspoon pepper

Serves 4–6

Preparation time: 10 minutes

Cooking time: 10 minutes

1 Put all the vegetables and chicken in a large saucepan and pour over enough water to cover. Add the bouquet garni, mace, lemon rind and juice and season with salt to taste. Bring to the boil over a low heat, skim, then cover and simmer for 1 hour, until the chicken is tender.

2 Take out the chicken and cut off about 250 g (8 oz) meat. Dice and set aside. Strain the stock and reserve 1.2 litres (2 pints). Leave to cool, then skim off any fat.

3 Melt the butter in a pan, stir in the flour and cook, stirring constantly, for 1 minute, without browning. Gradually stir in the reserved stock. Bring to the boil, stirring constantly. Simmer for 2 minutes, then add the diced chicken and heat through.

4 Blend the egg yolks and cream together. Remove the soup from the heat and stir in the cream mixture. Serve immediately.

1 large onion, chopped

2 celery sticks, chopped

2 large carrots, chopped

1 leek, chopped

1 x 1.25 kg (2½ lb) chicken

1 bouquet garni

1 mace blade

grated rind and juice of ½ lemon

salt

40 g (1½ oz) butter

40 g (1½ oz) plain flour

2 egg yolks

150 ml (¼ pint) double cream

Serves 6
Preparation time: 15 minutes, plus cooling
Cooking time: 1¼ hours

 The rest of the cooked chicken may be used for another dish, such as a pie, or as a pizza topping.

cream of chicken soup

1 Melt the butter in a large, heavy-based saucepan. Add the onion and cook over a low heat, stirring occasionally, for 8–10 minutes, until softened, but not coloured. Stir in the potatoes and watercress, cover and cook, stirring occasionally, for 3–5 minutes, until the watercress has just wilted.

2 Add the stock and season to taste with salt and pepper. Bring the soup to the boil, lower the heat and simmer for 6–8 minutes, until the potatoes are tender.

3 Process the soup in a blender or food processor, in batches if necessary, until smooth. Strain through a sieve and return to the pan. Add the cream, adjust the seasoning to taste and gently heat the soup without boiling.

4 Poach the quails' eggs in a pan of gently simmering water, until just set or cooked to taste. Remove the eggs with a slotted spoon and drain well on kitchen paper. Place 3 eggs in each serving bowl. Ladle the soup over the eggs and serve sprinkled with the grated Parmesan.

50 g (2 oz) butter

1 onion, finely chopped

250 g (8 oz) potatoes, cut into 1 cm (½ inch) cubes

300 g (10 oz) watercress, roughly chopped

900 ml (1½ pints) Chicken or Vegetable Stock (see pages 7 and 8)

300 ml (½ pint) single cream

12 quails' eggs

salt and pepper

50 g (2 oz) Parmesan cheese, finely grated, to serve

Serves 4

Preparation time: 5 minutes, plus cooling

Cooking time: 20–25 minutes

■ Once considered a luxury, quails' eggs are now widely available from most supermarkets.

speedy watercress soup with poached quails' eggs

fish & seafood soups

quick prawn & okra soup

1 Melt the butter in a saucepan. Add the onion and celery, cover and cook over a moderate heat until the onion softens, but has not browned. Add the stock and rice to the pan. Heat until just below boiling point, cover and cook gently for 20 minutes, or until the rice is tender.

2 Prepare the okra by cutting away the conical cap from the stalk end, then cut the pods into 1 cm (½ inch) slices.

3 Uncover the pan and add the tomatoes, okra, prawns and ham and cook, stirring frequently, for a further 5–8 minutes. Serve the soup in warmed bowls, garnished with small parsley leaves.

50 g (2 oz) butter

1 onion, finely chopped

200 g (7 oz) celery sticks, finely chopped

1 litre (1¾ pints) Fish Stock (see page 8)

50 g (2 oz) long-grain white rice

250 g (8 oz) okra

2 tomatoes, skinned (see page 9) and finely chopped

250 g (8 oz) cooked peeled prawns, defrosted if frozen

50 g (2 oz) cooked ham, cut into fine strips

small parsley leaves, to garnish

Serves 4–6
Preparation time: 15 minutes
Cooking time: 30–35 minutes

■ Okra, also known as bhindi and gumbo, are small, bright green, five-sided edible seed pods. They are featured in Indian and Caribbean cooking and are widely used in Louisiana and other southern states of the USA for the silky smooth finish they give to soups and stews.

1 Melt 25 g (1 oz) of the butter in a large, heavy-based saucepan. Add the carrots, celery and onion, cover and sweat over a low heat for 5–7 minutes. Break up the shells and legs of the lobster or crawfish and pack on top of the vegetables. Just cover the seafood with cold water and add the peppercorns, salt and parsley. Simmer over a low heat for 30–45 minutes. Strain through a sieve into a bowl and reserve.

2 Melt the remaining butter in the clean saucepan. Stir in the flour and cook, stirring constantly, for 2–3 minutes. Remove from the heat and gradually stir in the reserved stock. Return the pan to the heat and bring to the boil, stirring constantly. Taste and adjust the seasoning if necessary. Simmer for 5–6 minutes.

3 Add the chopped mint and stir in the double cream. Also add any reserved flakes of shellfish flesh. Heat through gently and serve with warmed French bread, if liked.

75 g (3 oz) butter

2 medium carrots, roughly chopped

1 celery stick, chopped

1 onion, roughly chopped

1 lobster or crawfish shell, legs and any scraps of leftover flesh (from seafood prepared for another recipe)

6 black peppercorns

pinch of salt

1 small bunch of parsley

50 g (2 oz) plain flour

2 teaspoons coarsely chopped mint

150 ml (¼ pint) double cream

warm French bread, to serve (optional)

Serves 4

Preparation time: 15 minutes, plus chilling

Cooking time: 40–45 minutes

lobster bisque

quick & easy prawn bisque

1 Melt the butter in a large, heavy-based saucepan. Add the carrot, onion and celery and cook, stirring occasionally, for 8–10 minutes, until softened and light golden. Increase the heat, add the prawns and cook for about 3–4 minutes, until the shells turn pink all over.

2 Add the wine and brandy, bring to the boil, lower the heat and simmer for 3–4 minutes, until the prawns are cooked. Remove the prawns and leave to cool slightly. When cool enough to handle, peel them, reserving their shells. Remove the black veins running down the back, chop the flesh and set aside.

3 Bring the liquid back to the boil and boil rapidly for 2–3 minutes, until reduced by one-third. Add the reserved prawn shells, together with the fish stock, bouquet garni and rice. Bring to the boil, reduce the heat and simmer gently for 15–20 minutes, until the rice is tender.

4 Remove and discard the bouquet garni. Process the soup, including the prawn shells, in a blender or food processor with three-quarters of the prawn meat. Strain through a fine sieve into a clean pan, pressing with the back of a ladle to push through as much liquid as possible. Add the cream and season to taste with salt, pepper and cayenne pepper. Add the reserved chopped prawns and heat gently for 1–2 minutes until hot, but not boiling. Serve sprinkled with chopped parsley and mango.

50 g (2 oz) butter

1 small carrot, finely chopped

½ small onion, finely chopped

½ celery stick, finely chopped

500 g (1 lb) raw prawns in their shells

250 ml (8 fl oz) dry white wine

2 tablespoons brandy

1.2 litres (2 pints) Fish Stock (see page 8)

1 bouquet garni

25 g (1 oz) long-grain rice

100 ml (3½ fl oz) double cream

pinch of cayenne pepper

salt and pepper

To Garnish:

4 tablespoons chopped parsley

1 small mango, peeled and finely chopped

Serves 4
Preparation time: 20 minutes
Cooking time: 30–40 minutes

■ Herbs used to make a bouquet garni may vary. A fairly standard combination is a bay leaf and 1 sprig each of marjoram, thyme and parsley tied together.

la bourride

1   First, make the aïoli. Crush the garlic and a pinch of salt using the back of a spoon. Beat in the egg yolks with an electric mixer until thick and creamy. Beat in the olive oil, a few drops at a time. When the mixture begins to thicken, add the oil in a thin stream, beating vigorously. Stir in the lemon juice, salt and pepper to taste. Cover and chill until required.

2   Put the leeks, onion, 2 of the garlic cloves and the potatoes in a large saucepan and place the fish on top. Cover with the stock and poach for about 10 minutes, or until the potatoes are tender and the fish is just cooked. Different varieties and thicknesses of fish cook at different speeds so be careful not to let it overcook and break up. With a slotted spoon, transfer the cooked fish, leeks and potatoes to a heated dish and keep warm.

3   Bring the remaining stock to the boil and reduce to one-third of the quantity. Remove from the heat and set aside to cool slightly. Gradually strain the stock into the aïoli, beating constantly. Then gently heat the soup in a saucepan, but do not let it boil.

4   Rub the inside of a frying pan with the remaining garlic clove and heat the olive oil. Fry the slices of bread in the oil until lightly browned on both sides and put a slice in the base of each soup bowl. Place the fish, leeks and potatoes on top, ladle over the soup and serve immediately.

2 leeks, thinly sliced

1 onion, thinly sliced

3 garlic cloves

500 g (1 lb) potatoes, thinly sliced

1.5 kg (3 lb) firm white fish, filleted and cut into bite-size pieces

1.8 litres (3 pints) Fish Stock (see page 8)

olive oil, for frying

1 stick French bread, thickly sliced

Aïoli:

3 garlic cloves, finely chopped

2 egg yolks

250 ml (8 fl oz) extra virgin olive oil

lemon juice

salt and pepper

Serves 8
Preparation time: 30 minutes
Cooking time: 20–25 minutes

500 g (1 lb) potatoes, cut into 1 cm (½ inch) cubes

1 onion, finely chopped

1 bay leaf

½ teaspoon chopped marjoram

600 ml (1 pint) water

500 g (1 lb) skinned smoked haddock fillet, coarsely chopped

¼ teaspoon ground nutmeg

450 ml (¾ pint) milk

freshly ground white pepper

To Garnish:

2 tablespoons finely chopped marjoram

croûtons (optional, see page 9)

1 Combine the potatoes, onion, bay leaf, marjoram and water in a saucepan. Bring the mixture to the boil, then lower the heat, cover and simmer for 5 minutes.

2 Add the haddock fillet, nutmeg and milk and season with white pepper to taste. Partially cover and simmer for 20 minutes. Remove and discard the bay leaf.

3 Serve the chowder in warmed soup bowls, garnished with finely chopped marjoram and croûtons, if using.

Serves 4–6
Preparation time: 10–15 minutes
Cooking time: 35 minutes

smoked haddock chowder

1 Place the rice in a small saucepan and cover with cold water. Bring to the boil, reduce the heat and simmer for 40–45 minutes, until tender. Drain and set aside.

2 Place the haddock, milk and bay leaf in a saucepan, bring to the boil, reduce the heat and simmer for 8–10 minutes, until just cooked. Remove the fish with a slotted spoon and set aside to cool. Remove the skin and any remaining bones and flake the flesh with a fork. Strain and reserve the milk.

3 Melt the butter in a heavy-based saucepan. Add the onion, leek, celery and garlic and cook over a low heat, stirring occasionally for 8–10 minutes, until softened, but not coloured. Add the thyme, stock and reserved milk. Season to taste with salt, pepper and nutmeg. Bring to the boil, reduce the heat and simmer for 10 minutes. Add the corn and cook for 5 minutes, then add the rice and flaked haddock and heat for a few minutes. Adjust the seasoning to taste.

4 To make the bacon croûtons, heat the oil in a large frying pan. Add the bacon and fry for 5–6 minutes until crisp. Remove with a slotted spoon, drain on kitchen paper and reserve. Add the bread cubes to the pan and cook, turning frequently, for 4–5 minutes, until crisp and golden brown. Drain on kitchen paper, then toss with the reserved bacon. Serve the soup sprinkled with the bacon croûtons and chopped parsley.

75 g (3 oz) wild rice

250 g (8 oz) smoked haddock

600 ml (1 pint) milk

1 bay leaf

50 g (2 oz) butter

1 large onion, chopped

1 leek, sliced

1 celery stick, chopped

1 garlic clove, crushed

1 tablespoon thyme leaves

900 ml (1½ pints) Chicken Stock (see page 7)

pinch of grated nutmeg

125 g (4 oz) sweetcorn, defrosted if frozen

salt and pepper

2 tablespoons chopped parsley, to garnish

Bacon Croûtons:

3 tablespoons olive oil

4 rashers of streaky bacon, rinded and cut into strips

2 slices of bread, crusts removed, cut into 1 cm (½ inch) cubes

Serves 4

Preparation time: 15 minutes

Cooking time: 1 hour 20 minutes

smoked haddock & corn soup with wild rice & bacon croûtons

speedy genoese fish soup

1 Melt the butter in a large saucepan. Add the onion and fry over a low heat, stirring occasionally, for 2–3 minutes, until softened, but not coloured. Add the celery and bacon to the pan and continue cooking over a low heat for a few more minutes.

2 Add the tomatoes, wine, stock and marjoram and season to taste with salt and pepper. Simmer for 10 minutes.

3 Add the fish and cook for 5 minutes. Finally, add the prawns and simmer for a further 2–3 minutes. Taste and adjust the seasoning, if necessary, and serve hot, garnished with chopped parsley. Offer warm rolls with the soup, if liked.

25 g (1 oz) butter

1 onion, chopped

3 celery sticks, chopped

50 g (2 oz) streaky bacon, rinded and chopped

425 g (14 oz) can chopped tomatoes

150 ml (¼ pint) dry white wine

300 ml (½ pint) Fish Stock (see page 8)

½ teaspoon chopped marjoram

500 g (1 lb) monkfish, cod or coley, boned, skinned and diced

125 g (4 oz) cooked peeled prawns

salt and pepper

2 tablespoons chopped parsley, to garnish

warm rolls, to serve (optional)

Serves 4–6

Preparation time: 20 minutes

Cooking time: 25–30 minutes

Garlic lovers can add a clove of garlic to this tasty soup to give extra flavour. Add the crushed or finely chopped garlic to the saucepan of melted butter with the chopped onion, then continue as above.

1 Cut the mackerel, whiting and haddock or cod into chunks. Heat the oil in a large, heavy-based saucepan. Add the garlic and onions and fry over a low heat, stirring occasionally, for 3–5 minutes, or until the onions are transparent, but not brown. Add the fish chunks and cook, uncovered, over a moderate heat, stirring occasionally, for 10 minutes.

2 Add the prawns and tomatoes. Dissolve the saffron strands in the hot fish stock and add to the pan, together with the bay leaf and parsley. Season with salt and pepper to taste. Stir and bring to the boil. Lower the heat, cover and simmer for 15 minutes, then add the mussels and continue cooking for a further 10 minutes, or until the fish is tender and flakes easily when tested with the tip of a knife.

3 Discard the bay leaf, parsley sprigs and any mussels that have not opened. Place the bread in a warmed soup tureen and ladle in the soup. Sprinkle with the chopped parsley before serving, if liked.

500 g (1 lb) mackerel fillets

500 g (1 lb) whiting fillets

500 g (1 lb) haddock or cod fillets

4 tablespoons olive oil

2 garlic cloves, finely chopped

2 onions, chopped

250 g (8 oz) raw peeled prawns

6 tomatoes, skinned (see page 9) and chopped

½ teaspoon saffron strands

1.5 litres (2½ pints) hot Fish Stock (see page 8)

1 bay leaf

3 parsley sprigs

10–12 live mussels, scrubbed and debearded

6–8 slices of French bread

salt and pepper

2 tablespoons finely chopped parsley, to garnish (optional)

Serves 6–8

Preparation time: 30–40 minutes

Cooking time: 30–35 minutes

bouillabaisse

1 Put the clams on a baking sheet in a preheated oven, 200°C (400°F), Gas Mark 6, for 2–3 minutes, until they open slightly, then remove and prise the shells apart. Open the shells over a bowl to catch all the clam juice. Snip off the inedible black-tipped necks (they look like a little tube), roughly chop the coral-coloured and pink flesh and leave the softer body meat whole.

2 Melt 25 g (1 oz) of the butter in a large saucepan. Add the bacon and cook for about 5 minutes, until the fat starts to run. Add the onions, cover and cook gently for 10 minutes. Add the celery, leeks, parsley, bay leaves and thyme and cook for a further 5 minutes. Add the reserved clam juice, the water, nutmeg and pepper to taste. Stir well, taste and season with salt if necessary. Add the potatoes and bring to the boil. Simmer gently for about 10 minutes, until the potatoes are almost tender.

3 Meanwhile, cream the flour with the remaining butter to a smooth paste and reserve. Add the clams to the saucepan and simmer very gently for 3–4 minutes. Do not boil or the clams will be tough and rubbery. Add a piece of the butter and flour paste to the saucepan, stirring well. When it has been fully incorporated, stir in a little more and continue until all the paste has been added. Stir for another 3–4 minutes until the soup thickens slightly.

4 Increase the heat briefly for 10 seconds, then remove from the heat. Add the Worcestershire sauce, stir and serve immediately, garnished with chopped parsley.

classic clam chowder

48–60 live clams in closed shells (discard any that do not shut immediately when sharply tapped)

40 g (1½ oz) butter

125 g (4 oz) smoked streaky bacon, rinded and diced

2 large onions, finely chopped

2 celery sticks, diced

1–2 leeks, sliced

2 tablespoons finely chopped parsley, plus extra to garnish

2 bay leaves

leaves from 1 thyme sprig

900 ml (1½ pints) water

ground nutmeg

4–5 medium potatoes, diced

2 tablespoons plain flour

1–2 teaspoons Worcestershire sauce

finely ground sea salt (optional) and pepper

Serves 6–8

Preparation time: 25–45 minutes

Cooking time: 35–40 minutes

mussel chowder

1 Heat the olive oil in a heavy-based saucepan. Add the bacon and cook over a moderate heat, stirring occasionally, until browned. Add the onions, celery and green pepper and cook, stirring frequently, for 5 minutes, or until the vegetables soften. Add the stock, potatoes, bay leaf and marjoram. Bring to the boil, then lower the heat, cover and simmer for 15–20 minutes, or until the potatoes are tender.

2 In a small bowl, blend the flour with 150 ml (¼ pint) of the milk. Whisk the mixture into the chowder, bring to the boil, stirring constantly, then gradually add the remaining milk. Season with salt and pepper to taste.

3 Lower the heat, add the mussels and simmer gently, stirring occasionally, for 5 minutes. Do not boil. Stir in the cream and pour the chowder into a warmed soup tureen. Garnish with chopped parsley, if using, and serve immediately with crusty French bread, if liked.

2 tablespoons olive oil

250 g (8 oz) smoked streaky bacon, rinded and chopped

2 onions, finely chopped

1 celery stick, finely chopped

1 green pepper, cored, deseeded and finely chopped

450 ml (¾ pint) Fish Stock (see page 8)

250 g (8 oz) potatoes, diced

1 bay leaf

½ teaspoon chopped marjoram

3 tablespoons plain flour

300 ml (½ pint) milk

500 g (1 lb) shelled mussels, defrosted if frozen

150 ml (¼ pint) single cream

salt and pepper

1 tablespoon finely chopped parsley, to garnish (optional)

crusty French bread, to serve (optional)

Serves 4–6	
Preparation time: 10–15 minutes	
Cooking time: 30 minutes	

■ Use the small plump European mussels – the large, green-lipped New Zealand mussels are not suitable for this chowder.

mussel soup with saffron, basil & spinach

1 Place the saffron in a small bowl, pour over the boiling water and set aside to infuse. Discard any mussels that are broken or do not shut immediately when sharply tapped with a knife. Place a large colander over a bowl.

2 Pour the white wine into a large saucepan. Bring the wine to the boil, add the mussels, cover with a tight-fitting lid and cook, shaking the pan frequently for 2–3 minutes, until the mussels have opened. Tip the mussels into the colander, discarding any that have not opened. Strain the mussel liquid through a muslin-lined sieve and set aside.

3 Heat the oil in a saucepan over a low heat. Add the shallots and garlic and cook over a low heat, stirring occasionally, for 5–6 minutes, until softened, but not coloured. Add the reserved mussel liquid, the cream, saffron and its infused liquid and heat to just below boiling point. Reduce the heat and add the spinach, half the basil and all the mussels. Cook gently for 2 minutes, without boiling, then remove from the heat. Stir in the remaining basil and serve at once.

pinch of saffron threads

125 ml (4 fl oz) boiling water

750 g (1½ lb) live mussels, scrubbed and debearded

175 ml (6 fl oz) dry white wine

2 tablespoons olive oil

2 shallots, finely chopped

1 garlic clove, finely chopped

200 ml (7 fl oz) double cream

175 g (6 oz) young leaf spinach

15 basil leaves, shredded

Serves 4
Preparation time: 30 minutes
Cooking time: 20 minutes

crab & rice soup

1 Cut the crab meat into 1 cm (½ inch) pieces. Heat the oil in a heavy-based saucepan. Add the crab meat and cook over a low heat until lightly browned. Add the onion and cook over a moderate heat, stirring constantly, for 5 minutes. Add the tomatoes, paprika, salt and boiling water. Lower the heat, cover and cook for about 45 minutes.

2 Meanwhile, pound the garlic cloves in a mortar with a pinch of salt and the parsley. Add the saffron strands and 2 tablespoons of the simmering stock. Stir the mixture well.

3 Add the garlic mixture and rice to the saucepan. Simmer, partially covered, for 20 minutes, or until the rice is tender. Turn off the heat and leave the soup to rest for 2–3 minutes. Stir and adjust the seasoning if necessary. Pour the soup into a warmed tureen and serve hot with croûtons.

500 g (1 lb) white crab meat

4 tablespoons olive oil

1 onion, chopped

250 g (8 oz) tomatoes, skinned (see page 9) and chopped

1 teaspoon paprika

½ teaspoon salt

1.8 litres (3 pints) boiling water

2 garlic cloves

2 parsley sprigs

3 saffron strands

250 g (8 oz) long-grain white rice

salt

croûtons, to garnish (see page 9)

Serves 6
Preparation time: 15 minutes
Cooking time: 1¼ hours

■ Use only white crab meat for this soup, as the brown meat has too delicate a texture. If fresh crab is not available, use the frozen and defrosted meat rather than canned, as it has a much better flavour.

crab soup

1   Pour the stock into a large saucepan. Add the ginger, tomatoes, chilli, rice wine or sherry, vinegar and sugar. Bring to the boil, cover the pan and simmer for about 10 minutes to allow the flavours to mingle and mellow.

2   Blend the cornflour to a paste with a little cold water, then pour it into the soup and stir to incorporate. Simmer, stirring, for 1–2 minutes until the soup thickens.

3   Add the crab meat, stir gently to mix, then heat through for 2–3 minutes. Taste and add salt and pepper if necessary. Serve piping hot, sprinkled with the sliced spring onions.

1 litre (1¾ pints) Chicken Stock (see page 7)

2.5 cm (1 inch) piece of fresh root ginger, peeled and very finely chopped

2 ripe tomatoes, skinned (see page 9), deseeded and very finely chopped

½ small red or green chilli, deseeded and very finely chopped

2 tablespoons rice wine or dry sherry

1 tablespoon rice wine vinegar, white wine vinegar or cider vinegar

½ teaspoon sugar

1 tablespoon cornflour

about 150 g (5 oz) white crab meat, defrosted and drained thoroughly, if frozen

salt and pepper

2 spring onions, finely sliced, to garnish

Serves 4–6

Preparation time: 10 minutes

Cooking time: about 20 minutes

vegetable

soups

quick & easy carrot soup

1 Melt the butter in a large saucepan. Add the onion and cook over a moderate heat, stirring frequently, for 5 minutes, until soft, but not golden. Add the carrots and turnips and cook, stirring constantly, for 1 minute. Pour in the water and stock. Stir, then add the potatoes and sugar and season with salt and pepper to taste. Bring to the boil, then lower the heat, cover and simmer for 25–30 minutes. Cool slightly.

2 Process the soup in a blender or food processor, in batches, if necessary, until smooth. Transfer the puréed soup to a clean saucepan.

3 Stir well and heat thoroughly without boiling. Taste and season with more salt and pepper if necessary. Just before serving, stir in the cream, if liked.

50 g (2 oz) butter

1 onion, chopped

500 g (1 lb) carrots, sliced

2 turnips, diced

900 ml (1½ pints) water

600 ml (1 pint) Vegetable Stock (see page 8)

250 g (8 oz) potatoes, sliced

pinch of sugar

3 tablespoons double cream (optional)

salt and pepper

Serves 6–8
Preparation time: 15 minutes
Cooking time: 30–35 minutes

1 Put the parsnips, carrots and onion in a large saucepan with the stock and season with salt and pepper, to taste. Bring to the boil, cover and simmer for 20 minutes, or until the vegetables are tender.

2 Remove from the heat and allow to cool slightly, then purée in a food processor or blender until smooth, or press through a fine sieve.

3 Return the soup to the cleaned saucepan and reheat. Serve hot in individual warmed soup bowls, garnished with a swirl of yogurt.

250 g (8 oz) parsnips, chopped

250 g (8 oz) carrots, chopped

1 onion, chopped

600 ml (1 pint) Chicken Stock (see page 7)

salt and pepper

natural yogurt, to garnish

| **Serves 4** |
| **Preparation time:** 15 minutes |
| **Cooking time:** about 30 minutes |

carrot & parsnip soup

50 g (2 oz) unsalted butter

500 g (1 lb) celery, chopped

500 g (1 lb) carrots, chopped

250 g (8 oz) dessert apples, peeled, cored and coarsely chopped

1.2 litres (2 pints) Vegetable Stock (see page 8)

1 teaspoon paprika

pinch of cayenne pepper

1 tablespoon chopped basil leaves

1 bay leaf

1 teaspoon grated fresh root ginger

salt and freshly ground white pepper

To Garnish:

chopped celery leaves

paprika

Serves 6	
Preparation time: 15 minutes	
Cooking time: 1 hour	

1 Melt the butter in a large saucepan. Add the celery, carrots and apples, cover with a tight-fitting lid and cook over a low heat, stirring occasionally, for 15 minutes.

2 Add the stock, paprika, cayenne pepper, basil leaves, bay leaf and ginger. Bring to the boil, lower the heat, partially cover and simmer for 40–45 minutes, or until the vegetables and apples are very soft.

3 Process the soup in a blender or food processor, in batches, if necessary, until smooth. Strain the soup through a sieve back into the clean saucepan. Season with salt and pepper to taste. Reheat the soup and serve it in warmed bowls, garnished with chopped celery leaves and a light sprinkling of paprika.

celery, carrot & apple soup

sweet potato soup

1 Dry-fry the bacon in a heavy-based frying pan over a low heat until the fat runs, then increase the heat and fry over a moderate heat until very crisp. Using tongs, transfer the bacon to kitchen paper to drain.

2 Add the butter to the fat in the frying pan. Add the onion, carrots, celery and bay leaf and fry over a low heat, stirring frequently, for 5–8 minutes. Transfer the mixture to a saucepan. Add the sweet potatoes, potatoes, stock, water and white wine. Bring the mixture to the boil, then lower the heat, cover and simmer for about 35–40 minutes, or until the vegetables are very tender. Remove and discard the bay leaf.

3 Process the mixture in a blender or food processor, in batches, if necessary, until smooth. Transfer the soup to a clean saucepan. Add the nutmeg, white pepper and salt to taste. Place the saucepan over a moderate heat and stir until the soup is hot. Serve the soup in warmed bowls. Crumble a little of the reserved bacon over each portion as a garnish.

4–6 rashers of smoked bacon, derinded

25 g (1 oz) butter

1 onion, chopped

2 carrots, sliced

2 celery sticks, chopped

1 bay leaf

750 g (1½ lb) sweet potatoes, sliced

250 g (8 oz) potatoes, sliced

1.2 litres (2 pints) Chicken Stock (see page 7)

150 ml (¼ pint) water

125 ml (4 fl oz) dry white wine

¼ teaspoon grated nutmeg

¼ teaspoon freshly ground white pepper

salt

Serves 6–8
Preparation time: 15 minutes
Cooking time: 50 minutes

1 Melt the butter in a large saucepan. Stir in the curry powder and cook, stirring constantly, for 2 minutes. Add the onions and parsnips and cook over a low heat, stirring occasionally, for 5 minutes. Add the stock and season with salt and pepper to taste.

2 Bring to the boil and cook for 25–30 minutes, until the vegetables are tender. Cool slightly.

3 Process the soup in a blender or food processor or rub through a sieve until smooth. Return to the pan and add the milk and cream. Heat gently, stirring constantly. Check the seasoning and serve immediately, garnished with diced apple.

50 g (2 oz) butter

1 teaspoon curry powder

2 large onions, chopped

750 g (1½ lb) parsnips, chopped

600 ml (1 pint) Chicken Stock (see page 7)

300 ml (½ pint) milk

150 ml (¼ pint) single cream

salt and freshly ground white pepper

1 red apple, cored, diced and tossed in lemon juice, to garnish

Serves 6–8
Preparation time: 10 minutes
Cooking time: 40–45 minutes

curried parsnip soup

1 To make the dumplings, place the porcini in a small bowl, cover with warm water and leave to soak for 30 minutes. Drain in a fine sieve, reserving the liquid. Rinse the mushrooms well in cold water, chop finely and set aside.

2 Melt the butter in a small pan over a low heat. Add the shallot and cook for 5–6 minutes, until softened, but not coloured. Spoon into a bowl, add the mushrooms, ricotta, Parmesan, egg yolks, flour and parsley and mix to form a soft dough. Season to taste. Cover and chill for 30–60 minutes. With lightly floured hands, form the dough into 30 small balls, roll in flour and place on a tray.

3 To make the soup, melt the butter in a pan over a low heat. Add the shallots or onion and garlic and cook, stirring frequently, for 5 minutes, until softened, but not coloured. Add the celeriac, cover and cook for 5–10 minutes, until the celeriac begins to soften. Add the stock and the reserved mushroom liquid. Bring to the boil, reduce the heat and simmer for 10–15 minutes.

4 Process the soup in a blender or food processor until smooth. Return the soup to the pan, stir in the cream or milk and season to taste. Reheat gently.

5 Bring a pan of lightly salted water to the boil. Add the dumplings and simmer for 3–4 minutes. Drain well and add to the soup just before serving. Serve the soup sprinkled with grated Parmesan cheese.

cream of celeriac soup with porcini dumplings

50 g (2 oz) butter

2 shallots or 1 onion, chopped

1 garlic clove, crushed

500 g (1 lb) celeriac, diced

900 ml (1½ pints) Chicken or Vegetable Stock (see pages 7 and 8)

300 ml (½ pint) single cream or milk

salt and pepper

finely grated Parmesan cheese, to garnish

Porcini Dumplings:

5 g (¼ oz) dried porcini mushrooms

25 g (1 oz) butter

1 shallot, very finely chopped

175 g (6 oz) ricotta cheese

25 g (1 oz) Parmesan cheese, finely grated

2 egg yolks, beaten

2 tablespoons plain flour, plus extra for dusting

1 tablespoon chopped parsley

Serves 4–6

Preparation time: 25 minutes, plus soaking

Cooking time: 30 minutes

root vegetable soup

1 Put all the diced vegetables and garlic into a 7 litre (12 pint) saucepan. Cover with the water and add the salt and butter. For the bouquet garni, tie the herbs, peppercorns and celery seeds loosely in muslin and add to the saucepan. Bring to the boil, lower the heat and simmer for about 40 minutes, until all the vegetables are tender.

2 Leave to cool slightly. Process the mixture in a blender or food processor, in batches and transfer the soup to a clean saucepan.

3 Reheat and serve with one or all of the suggested garnishes, if liked. The soup can be thinned if necessary with water, stock, single cream or tomato juice.

500 g (1 lb) potatoes, roughly diced

500 g (1 lb) carrots, roughly diced

500 g (1 lb) swede, roughly diced

500 g (1 lb) parsnips, roughly diced

500 g (1 lb) onions, roughly diced

500 g (1 lb) celeriac, roughly diced

2 large garlic cloves, crushed

2.5 litres (4 pints) water

2 teaspoons salt

125 g (4 oz) butter

Bouquet Garni:

2 bay leaves

1 thyme sprig

1 marjoram sprig

1 oregano sprig

2 teaspoons peppercorns

1 teaspoon celery seeds

Optional Garnishes:

250 g (8 oz) croûtons (see page 9) and 1 bunch spring onions, finely sliced

or 2 bunches of chives, finely snipped and 2 tablespoons chopped parsley

or 150 ml (¼ pint) double cream

| **Serves 8–12** |
| **Preparation time:** 45 minutes |
| **Cooking time:** 35–40 minutes |

1 Use a vegetable peeler to pare 1 courgette lengthways into thin ribbons. Set these aside for the garnish. Thickly slice the remaining courgettes and place in a colander. Sprinkle with salt and leave to stand for 10–15 minutes. Rinse in cold water, drain thoroughly and pat dry with kitchen paper.

2 Melt the butter in a large saucepan. Add the onions and cook over a moderate heat, stirring frequently, for 5 minutes, until soft, but not golden. Add the courgettes and cook, stirring frequently, for 5 minutes. Add the stock, ginger and nutmeg with pepper to taste. Bring to the boil and add the potatoes. Lower the heat, partially cover and simmer for 40–45 minutes, or until the vegetables are very soft.

3 Process the soup in a blender or food processor, in batches, until smooth. Transfer to a clean saucepan. Reheat gently and serve in warmed soup bowls. Garnish each portion with a swirl of cream, if liked, and a few of the reserved courgette ribbons sprinkled with a little coarsely ground black pepper.

1.5 kg (3 lb) small courgettes

50 g (2 oz) butter

250 g (8 oz) onions, chopped

1 litre (1¾ pints) Vegetable Stock (see page 8)

1 tablespoon grated fresh root ginger

pinch of grated nutmeg

375 g (12 oz) potatoes, chopped

salt and pepper

coarsely ground black pepper, to serve

150 ml (¼ pint) single cream, to garnish (optional)

Serves 6

Preparation time: 15 minutes

Cooking time: 55 minutes

courgette soup with fresh ginger

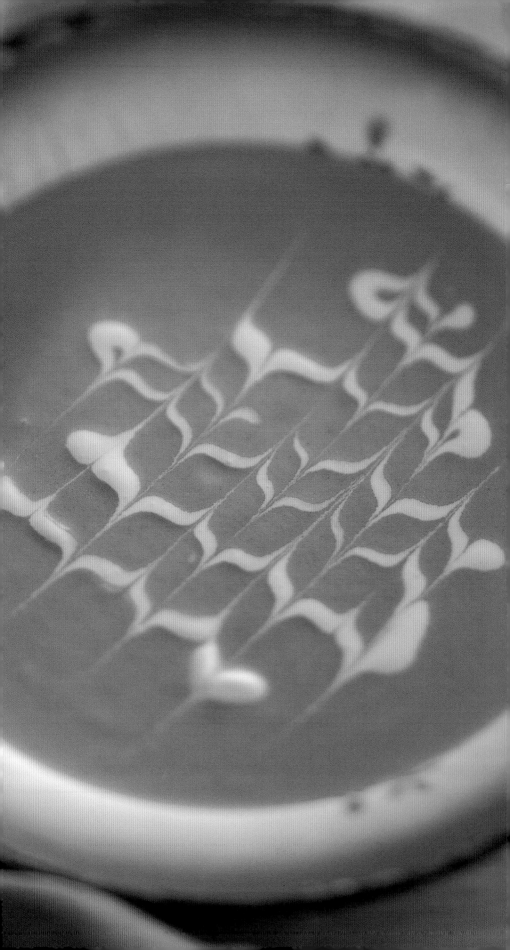

1 Melt the butter in a saucepan over a low heat. Add the onion and garlic and cook, stirring frequently, for 5–6 minutes, until the onion has softened. Stir in the courgettes and lemon rind and cook for a further 5–10 minutes, until tender.

2 Add the stock or water and mint, bring to the boil, then simmer for 5 minutes. Process the soup in a blender or food processor to a purée, then strain through a sieve.

3 Just before serving, reheat the soup to just below boiling point. Mix together the egg yolks and cream in a small bowl and whisk in a ladleful of the hot soup. Whisk this mixture back into the pan of soup, but do not allow the soup to boil or it will curdle. Season to taste with salt and pepper and serve in warmed individual bowls. To garnish, drizzle several lines of single cream across the surface of the soup. Drag a cocktail stick through the lines to give a feathered effect.

50 g (2 oz) butter

1 small onion, chopped

1–2 garlic cloves, crushed

750 g (1½ lb) courgettes, diced

finely grated rind of 1 lemon

600 ml (1 pint) Chicken Stock (see page 7) or water

2–3 tablespoons chopped mint

2 egg yolks

100 ml (3½ fl oz) double cream

salt and pepper

single cream, to garnish

Serves 4
Preparation time: 20 minutes
Cooking time: 25 minutes

courgette & mint soup

jerusalem artichoke soup

1 Place the lemon juice in a large bowl and add plenty of cold water. Peel the artichokes; reserve 2 and cut the rest into 1.5 cm (¾ inch) pieces. Drop the artichokes into the lemon water as you prepare them to prevent discoloration.

2 Melt the butter in a large, heavy-based saucepan. Add the onion, garlic, celery, thyme and lemon rind and cook over a low heat for 6–8 minutes, until softened, but not coloured. Drain the chopped artichokes and add to the pan, with the stock. Season to taste with salt and pepper, bring to the boil, reduce the heat and simmer for about 15 minutes, until the artichokes are tender.

3 To prepare the artichoke crisps, drain the 2 whole artichokes, slice thinly and dry well on kitchen paper. Heat some oil in a deep pan to 180–190°C (350–375°F), or until a cube of bread browns in 30 seconds. Fry the artichoke slices in batches until crisp and golden. Drain them well on kitchen paper.

4 Process the soup in a blender or food processor, in batches if necessary. Strain through a sieve and return to the pan. Add the cream or milk and a little water if too thick, season to taste with salt and pepper and reheat gently. Stir in the finely grated Parmesan and serve sprinkled with the artichoke crisps.

finely grated rind and juice of 1 small lemon

625 g (1¼ lb) Jerusalem artichokes

50 g (2 oz) butter

1 onion, chopped

1 garlic clove, crushed

1 celery stick, chopped

1 lemon thyme sprig, leaves removed from stalk

1 litre (1¾ pints) Chicken or Vegetable Stock (see pages 7 and 8)

oil, for frying

175 ml (6 fl oz) single cream or milk

3 tablespoons finely grated Parmesan cheese

salt and pepper

Serves 4
Preparation time: 25 minutes
Cooking time: 30 minutes

■ Instead of making the Jerusalem artichoke crisps, toast 50 g (2 oz) hazelnuts, leave to cool, then coarsely grind or chop them. Sprinkle over the soup to serve.

1 Melt the butter in a large saucepan. Add the onion, celery and cauliflower, cover and cook over a moderate heat, stirring frequently, for 5–8 minutes. Stir in the stock with 450 ml (¾ pint) of the milk. Bring to the boil, then lower the heat, cover and simmer for 25 minutes.

2 Process the soup in a blender or food processor, in batches, until smooth. Pour the soup into a clean saucepan. Stir in half of the remaining milk. Season with salt and pepper to taste and stir in the nutmeg.

3 In a small bowl mix the cornflour with the remaining milk to a smooth paste and add it to the soup. Bring to the boil, stirring constantly. Lower the heat and simmer for 2 minutes. Serve immediately, in warmed soup bowls. Garnish each portion with a sprinkling of finely chopped parsley.

50 g (2 oz) butter

1 onion, chopped

1 celery stick, chopped

1 large cauliflower, about 750 g (1½ lb), cut into small florets

900 ml (1½ pints) Vegetable Stock (see page 8)

750 ml (1¼ pints) milk

1 teaspoon grated nutmeg

1 tablespoon cornflour

salt and freshly ground white pepper

finely chopped parsley, to garnish

Serves 6–8
Preparation time: 15 minutes
Cooking time: 35 minutes

no-fuss cauliflower soup

curried cream of broccoli soup

1 Strip off all the tough stems and leaves from the broccoli. Cut off the stalks, peel them and cut them into 2.5 cm (1 inch) pieces. Break the florets into very small pieces and set them aside.

2 Melt the butter in a large saucepan. Add the onion and broccoli stalks, cover and cook over a moderate heat, stirring frequently, for 5 minutes. Add the reserved florets, potato, curry powder and stock. Bring to the boil. Partially cover and cook for 5 minutes. Using a slotted spoon remove 6 or more broccoli florets for the garnish, if liked, and set aside. Season well with salt and pepper. Continue to cook over a moderate heat for 20 minutes, or until all the vegetables are soft.

3 Process the soup in a blender or food processor, in batches, if necessary, until smooth. Pour the soup into a clean saucepan. Add the cream and heat thoroughly without allowing the soup to boil. Serve in warmed soup bowls, garnishing each portion with the reserved florets, if using.

1 kg (2 lb) broccoli

50 g (2 oz) butter

1 onion, chopped

1 large potato, quartered

1 tablespoon medium hot curry powder

1.5 litres (2½ pints) Vegetable Stock (see page 8)

150 ml (¼ pint) single cream

salt and pepper

Serves 6
Preparation time: 10–15 minutes
Cooking time: 25 minutes

bortsch

1 Place the beetroot in a saucepan, cover with plenty of cold water and add 1 tablespoon of salt. Bring to the boil, lower the heat, cover and simmer steadily for 35–45 minutes. Drain, discarding the liquid, then rinse the beetroot under cold water, dry with kitchen paper and slip off the skins.

2 Grate the beetroot into a large saucepan. Add the tomatoes, beef stock, cabbage, 2 teaspoons of salt, the bay leaf, caraway seeds, peppercorns, vinegar and sugar. Stir well. Bring to the boil, lower the heat, cover the pan and simmer gently for about 1½ hours.

3 Remove and discard the bay leaf. Add the potatoes to the soup and continue simmering until they are tender, but not too soft. Serve the soup hot, in warmed soup bowls, and garnish each portion with a teaspoon of soured cream, if using.

4 raw beetroot

4 tomatoes, skinned (see page 9) and chopped

1.2 litres (2 pints) Beef Stock (see page 7)

3 large cabbage leaves, coarsely shredded

1 bay leaf

½ teaspoon caraway seeds

6 black peppercorns, crushed

5 tablespoons red wine vinegar

2 tablespoons sugar

6 small potatoes

salt

6 teaspoons soured cream, to garnish (optional)

Serves 6	
Preparation time:	15 minutes
Cooking time:	about 3 hours

75 g (3 oz) butter

1 large onion, finely chopped

500 g (1 lb) mushrooms, finely chopped

25 g (1 oz) plain flour

900 ml (1½ pints) Chicken Stock (see page 7)

125 ml (4 fl oz) dry Madeira

150 ml (¼ pint) double cream

salt and pepper

chopped parsley, to garnish

1 Melt the butter in a large saucepan. Add the onion and cook over a low heat, stirring frequently, for 20 minutes, or until evenly browned. Add the mushrooms and cook for 2 minutes.

2 Stir in the flour and cook for 1 minute. Gradually stir in the stock, then season with salt and pepper to taste. Bring to the boil, cover and simmer for 10 minutes.

3 Stir in the Madeira and cream and heat through gently. Serve immediately, garnished with parsley.

Serves 4–6
Preparation time: 5 minutes
Cooking time: 40 minutes

mushroom soup with madeira

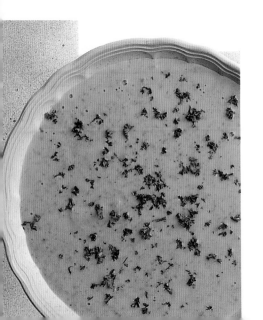

1 To make the Parmesan dumplings, place all the ingredients in a bowl and mix to form a firm paste. Season to taste with salt, pepper and nutmeg. Cover and chill in the refrigerator for 30–60 minutes. With lightly floured hands, form the mixture into 24 small balls, roll in flour and place on a tray.

2 To make the soup, heat the oil in a saucepan. Add the garlic and onions and cook over a low heat for 5 minutes, until softened, but not coloured. Cover with a tight-fitting lid and cook for 30–35 minutes, until very soft, but do not allow the garlic or onions to colour.

3 Add the potatoes, bay leaf, thyme, saffron, stock and milk and season to taste with salt and pepper. Bring to the boil, reduce the heat and simmer for 20–30 minutes. Add the spinach and cook for 1–2 minutes, until it has wilted.

4 Process the soup in a blender or food processor, in batches if necessary. Strain through a sieve into a clean pan and reheat. Bring a small pan of lightly salted water to the boil and drop in the dumplings. Cook for 3–4 minutes, drain well and serve in the soup. Serve sprinkled with coarsely ground black pepper.

5 tablespoons olive oil

2 small heads of garlic, peeled

250 g (8 oz) onions, sliced

500 g (1 lb) potatoes, diced

1 bay leaf

1 thyme sprig

pinch of saffron threads

1.2 litres (2 pints) Chicken or Vegetable Stock (see pages 7 and 8)

600 ml (1 pint) milk

250 g (8 oz) fresh spinach, tough stems removed, finely shredded

salt and pepper

coarsely ground black peppercorns, to serve

Parmesan Dumplings:

175 g (6 oz) ricotta cheese

25 g (1 oz) butter, softened

25 g (1 oz) Parmesan cheese, finely grated

1 teaspoon finely grated lemon rind

2 tablespoons plain flour, plus extra for rolling

2 egg yolks, beaten

freshly grated nutmeg

Serves 4–6
Preparation time: 30 minutes
Cooking time: 55 minutes

garlic & spinach soup with parmesan dumplings

tomato chowder

1 Combine all the ingredients, except the cheese, in a large saucepan. Stir well. Bring to the boil over a moderate heat, stirring constantly, then lower the heat and simmer for 3 minutes.

2 Ladle the soup into warmed ovenproof bowls, sprinkle with the cheese and place under a preheated hot grill for 3–5 minutes, until the cheese is bubbling. Serve the chowder immediately.

300 g (10 oz) can condensed tomato soup

425 g (14 oz) can tomatoes, sieved

325 g (11 oz) can sweetcorn, drained

1 tablespoon Worcestershire sauce

3–6 drops of Tabasco sauce

1 teaspoon chopped oregano

½ teaspoon sugar

125 g (4 oz) Cheddar cheese, grated

Serves 4–6

Preparation time: 5 minutes

Cooking time: about 10 minutes

1   Discard all but the top 6–8 cm (2½–3½ inches) of the asparagus spears, as the lower part may make the soup bitter. Cut the remainder into 2.5 cm (1 inch) lengths. Reserve a few 1 cm (½ inch) tips for garnishing and cook these separately for 10 minutes in a little boiling, salted water.

2   Bring the stock to the boil. Add the asparagus, peas or spinach and sugar and season to taste with salt and pepper. Bring back to the boil, lower the heat and simmer until the vegetables are tender. Cool slightly, then process the vegetables and stock in a food processor or press the soup through a sieve.

3   Melt the butter in the clean saucepan, stir in the flour and add the asparagus purée. Bring to the boil, stirring and adding the milk. Ladle into a warmed tureen or individual soup bowls. Stir in the cream, add a few asparagus tips to garnish and serve immediately.

20 asparagus spears

900 ml (1½ pints) Chicken Stock (see page 7)

250 g (8 oz) peas or spinach, chopped

1 teaspoon sugar

25 g (1 oz) butter

25 g (1 oz) plain flour

150 ml (¼ pint) milk

6 tablespoons double cream

salt and pepper

Serves 6	
Preparation time:	15 minutes
Cooking time:	30 minutes

asparagus soup

vichyssoise •

mint, cucumber & green pea soup •

chilled cucumber & yellow pepper soup •

simple chilled potato chowder •

chilled prawn & pea soup •

carrot & orange soup •

no-cook gazpacho •

white gazpacho •

chilled tomato soup •

tomato soup with basil •

chilled tomato, strawberry & rhubarb soup •

fig soup with cattucini •

apricot, orange & cardamom soup •

watermelon & lime soup •

chilled fennel & apple soup •

chilled
soups

vichyssoise

1 Melt the butter in a saucepan. Add the onions and cook over a low heat, stirring frequently, for 10 minutes, until softened, but not browned.

2 Add the leeks and potatoes and toss well. Stir in the stock, add the bouquet garni and season with salt and pepper to taste. Bring to the boil, cover and simmer, stirring occasionally, for 30–40 minutes. Remove and discard the bouquet garni and cool slightly.

3 Process the soup in a blender or food processor until smooth. Pour into a soup tureen and leave until cool. Stir in the cream. Chill for 3–4 hours. Garnish with chives and croûtons just before serving.

50 g (2 oz) butter

2 large onions, chopped

4 large leeks, white parts only, sliced

4 large potatoes, diced

1.2 litres (2 pints) Chicken Stock (see page 7)

1 bouquet garni

150 ml (¼ pint) double cream

salt and freshly ground white pepper

To Garnish:

2 tablespoons snipped chives

croûtons (see page 9)

Serves 6
Preparation time: 15 minutes, plus chilling
Cooking time: 45–50 minutes

1 Melt the butter in a large saucepan. Add the cucumber and cook over a moderate heat, stirring occasionally, for 5 minutes. Add the peas, sugar, pepper and 2 tablespoons of the mint. Pour in the stock. Bring to the boil, then add the potatoes. Lower the heat, partially cover and simmer gently for about 20 minutes, or until the potatoes are tender.

2 Purée the soup in a blender or food processor, in batches, if necessary, until smooth. Transfer the soup to a bowl. Season with salt to taste. Cool, cover the bowl closely and chill in the refrigerator for at least 3 hours.

3 Just before serving fold in the chilled cream. Serve in chilled bowls, garnishing each portion with a little of the remaining mint, if liked.

mint, cucumber & green pea soup

50 g (2 oz) butter

500 g (1 lb) cucumbers, peeled, deseeded and cut into 1 cm (½ inch) pieces

250 g (8 oz) shelled fresh or frozen peas, defrosted

pinch of sugar

¼ teaspoon white pepper

3 tablespoons finely chopped mint

1.2 litres (2 pints) Chicken or Vegetable Stock (see pages 7 and 8)

175 g (6 oz) potatoes, chopped

salt

150 ml (¼ pint) double cream, chilled

Serves 6

Preparation time: 15 minutes, plus chilling

Cooking time: 25–30 minutes

■ This soup is equally delicious served hot. After processing to a purée, return the soup to a clean saucepan, add the cream and reheat gently without boiling. Serve in warmed bowls, garnishing each portion with a little chopped mint.

chilled cucumber & yellow pepper soup

1 Cut off a third of 1 cucumber. Cut into fine dice and reserve for the garnish. Roughly chop the remaining cucumber.

2 Place the chopped cucumber and garlic in a blender or food processor and process until very smooth. Pour into a bowl and stir in the yogurt. Add enough iced water to make a smooth soup. Season to taste with salt and pepper. Stir in the mint, cover and chill thoroughly.

3 Chop 1 yellow pepper into fine dice, mix with the reserved cucumber and set aside for the garnish. Chop the remaining pepper and place in a small saucepan with the lime or lemon juice, sugar, 75 ml (3 fl oz) water and a pinch of cayenne. Bring to the boil, reduce the heat and simmer for 10–15 minutes, until the pepper is soft and the liquid has reduced. Remove from the heat and process in a blender or food processor. Strain the purée through a sieve into a bowl. Leave to cool, cover and chill in the refrigerator.

4 Ladle the soup into individual bowls. Sprinkle with the diced yellow pepper and cucumber and drizzle the yellow pepper purée over.

2 cucumbers, peeled and deseeded

1 garlic clove, crushed

250 ml (8 fl oz) natural yogurt, preferably Greek yogurt

125 ml (4 fl oz) iced water

4 tablespoons chopped mint

2 yellow peppers, cored and deseeded

2 tablespoons lime or lemon juice

1 tablespoon sugar

cayenne pepper

salt and pepper

Serves 4–6

Preparation time: 30 minutes, plus chilling

Cooking time: 10–15 minutes

As a variation, substitute fresh dill for the mint and garnish the soup with 125 g (4 oz) fresh white crab meat.

simple chilled potato chowder

1 Melt the butter in a large saucepan. Add the potatoes and onions and cook, stirring frequently, for 10 minutes, until the onions are softened slightly.

2 Add the mushroom soup, milk and mustard and season with salt and pepper to taste. Stir well. Heat gently until the soup begins to simmer. Pour the soup into a bowl and leave to cool. Cover the bowl tightly and chill the chowder in the refrigerator for at least 3 hours.

3 Serve in chilled bowls, garnishing each portion with a little cottage cheese, if using, a few snipped chives and a light dusting of paprika.

25 g (1 oz) butter

5 potatoes, diced

3 onions, sliced

475 g (15 oz) can cream of mushroom soup

900 ml (1½ pints) milk

1 teaspoon English mustard

salt and pepper

To Garnish:

2 tablespoons cottage cheese (optional)

a few snipped chives

paprika

Serves 6
Preparation time: 10 minutes, plus chilling
Cooking time: about 20 minutes

1 Pod the peas if using fresh, reserving the pods. Peel the prawns, reserving the shells. Cover the prawns and refrigerate. Place the prawn shells and pea pods, if available, in a large saucepan with the onion, garlic and stock. Bring to the boil, reduce the heat and simmer gently for 15 minutes.

2 Strain the stock into a clean pan, add the peas and season with salt, pepper and nutmeg. Bring back to the boil, reduce the heat and simmer until the peas are tender. Purée the mixture in a blender or food processor until smooth. Pour into a bowl, adjust the seasoning to taste, stir in the wine, if using, soured cream and lemon juice. Cool, cover the bowl and chill thoroughly.

3 Pour the soup into individual bowls and divide the prawns between them. Add a spoonful of soured cream and some salmon roe, if using. Sprinkle with chives and serve with Melba toast or French bread, if liked.

750 g (1½ lb) fresh young peas in the pod or 250 g (8 oz) frozen peas, defrosted

250 g (8 oz) cooked small prawns in their shells

1 onion, chopped

1 garlic clove, crushed

600 ml (1 pint) Chicken Stock (see page 7) or water

pinch of grated nutmeg

150 ml (¼ pint) dry white wine (optional)

150 ml (¼ pint) soured cream

1 tablespoon lemon juice

salt and pepper

To Serve:

soured cream (optional)

4 teaspoons salmon roe (optional)

2 tablespoons snipped chives

Melba toast or French bread (optional)

Serves 4

Preparation time: 30 minutes, plus chilling

Cooking time: 30 minutes

chilled prawn & pea soup

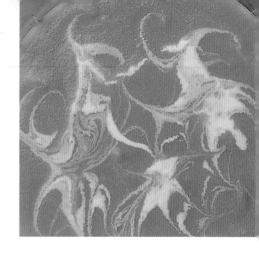

carrot & orange soup

1 Melt the butter in a large saucepan. Add the carrots and onion and cook over a low heat, stirring frequently, for 10 minutes, without browning.

2 Add the stock, sugar and salt and pepper to taste. Bring to the boil, cover and simmer for 1 hour, or until the carrots are tender. Leave to cool slightly.

3 Sieve or process the soup in a blender or food processor until smooth. Pour into a soup tureen and stir in the orange rind and juice. Leave to cool, then cover tightly and chill in the refrigerator for several hours. Just before serving, stir in the cream.

25 g (1 oz) butter

500 g (1 lb) carrots, sliced

1 onion, chopped

900 ml (1½ pints) Chicken Stock (see page 7)

pinch of sugar

grated rind of 1 orange

juice of 4 oranges

150 ml (¼ pint) single cream, chilled

salt and pepper

Serves 6

Preparation time: 15 minutes, plus chilling

Cooking time: 1¼ hours

■ Make sure that the oranges are at room temperature before squeezing them, as this increases the quantity of juice they yield.

1   Combine the garlic and salt in a mortar and pound with a pestle until smooth. Alternatively place the garlic and salt on a board and crush the garlic with the flat blade of a large knife. Place the bread in a bowl and cover with cold water. Soak for 5 seconds, then drain the bread, squeezing out the moisture.

2   Set aside a quarter of the tomatoes, onions, cucumber and peppers for the garnish. Place the remaining vegetables in a blender or food processor. Add the garlic paste, bread and oil and process the mixture until it is very smooth. Pour the mixture into a bowl and stir in the vinegar and water with pepper to taste. Cover tightly and chill in the refrigerator for at least 3 hours.

3   Chop the reserved vegetables finely and place them in small bowls. Serve the soup very cold, in chilled individual bowls. Add a selection of the vegetable accompaniments to the soup, as liked, and offer the remainder in their small bowls so that they can be added to taste. Croûtons may also be served.

no-cook gazpacho

2 garlic cloves, roughly chopped

¼ teaspoon salt

3 thick slices of white bread, crusts removed

1 kg (2 lb) tomatoes, skinned (see page 9) and coarsely chopped

2 onions, coarsely chopped

½ large cucumber, peeled, deseeded and coarsely chopped

2 large green peppers, cored, deseeded and coarsely chopped

5 tablespoons olive oil

4 tablespoons white wine vinegar

1 litre (1¾ pints) water

pepper

croûtons (optional, see page 9), to garnish

Serves 6

Preparation time: 10–15 minutes, plus chilling

1 Place the bread in a bowl, cover with cold water and set aside to soak for 5 minutes. Squeeze the water out of the bread.

2 Place the almonds and garlic in a blender or food processor, then process until very finely ground and almost paste-like. With the motor running, gradually add the bread and process until smooth. Then gradually add the oil in a thin stream. When all the oil has been incorporated, add the vinegar, scraping the mixture down the sides of the bowl if necessary. Pour in 300 ml (½ pint) of the iced water and process briefly to combine.

3 Strain through a sieve into a large bowl, pressing with the back of a ladle to extract as much liquid as possible. Stir in more iced water to make a thin soup and season to taste with salt. Cover tightly and chill thoroughly.

4 Just before serving, stir the soup well as it may have separated slightly. Ladle the soup into chilled individual bowls and garnish with a few halved grapes.

4 slices of day-old white bread, crusts removed

125 g (4 oz) blanched almonds, coarsely chopped

1–2 garlic cloves, chopped

100 ml (3½ oz) extra virgin olive oil

2–3 tablespoons sherry vinegar

1 litre (1¾ pints) iced water

salt

250 g (8 oz) white seedless grapes, halved, to garnish

Serves 4

Preparation time: 10–15 minutes, plus chilling

white gazpacho

1 Heat the olive oil and butter in a heavy-based saucepan. Add the onion and garlic and cook over a low heat, stirring frequently, for 3–5 minutes, or until softened, but not golden. Add the tomatoes and cook, stirring frequently, for 3 minutes.

2 Add the stock, oregano, caster sugar, celery salt, nutmeg and Worcestershire sauce and season with salt and pepper to taste. Stir well and bring to the boil. Lower the heat, partially cover and simmer for 45 minutes. Cool slightly.

3 Purée the soup in a blender or food processor then transfer to a bowl. Stir in the soured cream and allow the soup to cool completely, then cover the bowl tightly and chill in the refrigerator for at least 3 hours.

4 Meanwhile, place a Spanish olive in each section of a 6-cube ice tray and top up with cold water. Freeze until solid. Serve the soup in chilled bowls, with an olive-filled ice cube on each serving. Garnish with parsley, if liked.

2 tablespoons olive oil

25 g (1 oz) butter

1 large onion, chopped

1 garlic clove, chopped

750 g–1 kg (1½–2 lb) tomatoes, skinned (see page 9) and coarsely chopped

900 ml (1½ pints) Chicken Stock (see page 7)

1 teaspoon chopped oregano

1½ teaspoons caster sugar

¼ teaspoon celery salt

pinch of ground nutmeg

1 tablespoon Worcestershire sauce

150 ml (¼ pint) soured cream

salt and pepper

To Garnish:

6 Spanish olives

chopped parsley (optional)

Serves 6

Preparation time: 20–25 minutes, plus chilling

Cooking time: 50–55 minutes

---

chilled tomato soup

tomato soup with basil

1 Melt the butter in a large saucepan. Add the onion and cook over a low heat, stirring frequently, for 5 minutes, until softened, but not coloured. Add the tomatoes and cook, stirring frequently, for 2 minutes.

2 Add the stock and bring to the boil. Lower the heat, add the sugar and season with salt and pepper to taste. Simmer over a low heat for 20 minutes.

3 Process briefly in a blender or food processor, or pass through a medium food mill. Adjust the seasoning, cool, and chill well. About 10 minutes before serving, stir in the chopped basil. Garnish with a swirl of cream and a sprinkling of chives.

50 g (2 oz) butter

1 large mild onion, chopped

750 g (1½ lb) tomatoes, skinned (see page 9) and chopped

600 ml (1 pint) hot Chicken Stock (see page 7)

pinch of sugar

3 tablespoons chopped basil

salt and pepper

To Garnish:

1 tablespoon single cream

1 tablespoon snipped chives

Serves 4

Preparation time: 10 minutes, plus chilling

Cooking time: 30 minutes

chilled tomato, strawberry & rhubarb soup

1 Put the tomatoes, strawberries and rhubarb into a 4.5 litre (8 pint) stainless steel or enamel pan and cover with the stock. Add the salt and pepper. Bring to the boil, lower the heat and simmer for about 10 minutes, until the fruit is soft.

2 Press through a fine sieve into a bowl. Rub and scrape the pulp through until no more than a tablespoon of debris remains in the sieve. Cool, then chill in the refrigerator, preferably overnight.

3 Serve in chilled bowls with a swirl of cream, if using, and top with peppered strawberry slices with a sprinkling of chives.

1 kg (2 lb) ripe tomatoes, halved and seeded

750 g (1½ lb) strawberries, hulled, and halved

1 kg (2 lb) pink rhubarb, chopped

1.75 litres (3 pints) Chicken Stock (see page 7)

2 teaspoons salt

3–4 teaspoons freshly ground white pepper

300 ml (½ pint) double cream (optional), to serve

To Garnish:

250 g (8 oz) strawberries, hulled, sliced and lightly peppered

2 tablespoons snipped chives

Serves 12

Preparation time: 30 minutes, plus chilling

Cooking time: 10–15 minutes

1 Set aside 4 of the figs. Place the remaining figs in a large saucepan with the remaining ingredients. Bring to the boil, lower the heat and simmer for 2 minutes. Remove from the heat, cover, and leave to infuse for 10 minutes.

2 If using a vanilla pod, discard the pod, scraping the seeds into the soup, and discard the cinnamon stick and orange rind. Process the soup in a blender or food processor. Strain through a sieve and return to the pan.

3 Add the reserved figs and bring to the boil. Reduce the heat, cover and simmer for 5–7 minutes until tender, turning the figs over after 2–3 minutes. Transfer the poached figs and soup to a bowl, taste and add more honey or lemon juice if required. Cool, cover and chill thoroughly.

4 Just before serving, remove the figs with a slotted spoon and cut each fig into wedges. Ladle the soup into chilled bowls and garnish with the fig wedges. Serve with the cattucini biscuits and a spoonful of mascarpone cheese.

16 small figs, preferably black

1 vanilla pod, split lengthways, or a few drops of vanilla essence

5 cm (2 inch) piece of cinnamon stick

2 strips of pared orange rind

250 ml (8 fl oz) water

375 ml (13 fl oz) red wine

2 tablespoons clear honey

2 tablespoons fresh lemon juice

To Serve:

cattucini or other Italian biscuits

mascarpone cheese

Serves 4
Preparation time: 15 minutes, plus chilling
Cooking time: 15 minutes

fig soup with cattucini

apricot, orange & cardamom soup

1 Pare the rind from the oranges, making sure that none of the bitter white pith is attached, and cut into very thin strips. Bring a small saucepan of water to the boil, add the orange rind and simmer for 2 minutes. Remove from the heat, refresh in cold water and leave to drain.

2 Squeeze the juice from the oranges and pour into a saucepan. Add the sugar and crushed cardamom seeds. Stir over a medium heat until the sugar has dissolved, then set aside to cool.

3 Place the apricots in a blender or food processor with the orange syrup and blend until smooth. Strain through a sieve into a bowl, cover and chill thoroughly.

4 Ladle the soup into chilled soup bowls. Top each serving with a spoonful of mascarpone cheese or whipped cream and decorate with the strips of orange rind.

2 large oranges

125 g (4 oz) sugar

2 green cardamom pods, seeds removed and crushed

750 g (1½ lb) fresh apricots, halved, pitted and chopped

mascarpone cheese or softly whipped cream, to serve

Serves 4

Preparation time: 25 minutes, plus chilling

Cooking time: 10 minutes

watermelon & lime soup

1 Using a melon baller, scoop out 20–24 balls of watermelon flesh, cover and set aside in the refrigerator. Discard the skin from the remaining melon, chop the flesh roughly and place in a sieve set over a bowl. Push the flesh though the sieve, extracting as much juice as possible. Discard the melon seeds.

2 Place the sugar, water and lime rind in a small saucepan over a low heat. Stir until the sugar has dissolved, bring to the boil and simmer for 2–3 minutes. Remove from the heat and leave to cool slightly. Pour the lime juice and half of the syrup into the sieved melon and stir to mix. Taste and add more syrup or lime juice if required. Cover and chill.

3 To serve, ladle the soup into individual bowls or glasses. Add the reserved melon balls and serve.

2.5 kg (5 lb) slice of watermelon

125 g (4 oz) caster sugar

250 ml (8 fl oz) water

finely grated rind and juice of 1 lime, plus extra to taste

soured cream or crème fraîche, to serve (optional)

Serves 4
Preparation time: 15 minutes, plus chilling
Cooking time: 2–3 minutes

2 tablespoons olive oil

125 g (4 oz) onion, finely chopped

1 head fennel, about 300–375 g (10–12 oz), cut into 2.5 cm (1 inch) dice

250 g (8 oz) potatoes, cubed

1 garlic clove, crushed

1 small bay leaf

1 teaspoon fennel seeds, tied in a piece of muslin

2–3 tablespoons lemon juice

600 ml (1 pint) Chicken Stock (see page 7)

300 ml (½ pint) unsweetened apple juice

salt and pepper

To Garnish:

300 ml (¼ pint) single cream or 200 ml (7 fl oz) natural yogurt, chilled

2 Cox's apples, peeled, cored, finely sliced and sprinkled with lemon juice

2 tablespoons chopped fennel fronds

Serves 5–6

Preparation time: 45 minutes, plus chilling

Cooking time: 35–40 minutes

---

1 Heat the oil in a large saucepan. Add the onion, cover and cook over a low heat, stirring occasionally, for about 8–10 minutes, until softened, but not coloured. Add the fennel and potatoes and cook, stirring occasionally, for a further 10 minutes. Add the garlic, bay leaf, fennel seeds, lemon juice, stock and apple juice. Season to taste with salt and pepper. Bring to the boil and simmer for approximately 15 minutes, until the potatoes are very tender.

2 Strain into a bowl through a sieve, reserving the vegetable pulp. Leave to cool. As it cools surplus oils will rise to the surface of the liquid, skim these off and discard.

3 Process the vegetable pulp in a blender or food processor until smooth. Stir the purée into the cooled, skimmed liquid. Cover and chill in the refrigerator, preferably overnight.

4 Before serving, whisk in the chilled cream or yogurt. Add a slice of apple to each serving and sprinkle with a little chopped fennel.

chilled fennel & apple soup

index